THE VOID

SHANKAR

Made with ♥ on the Notion Press Platform
www.notionpress.com

To my father, Siva, whose wisdom and guidance shaped my path.
To my mother, Chitra, and my wife, Archana, for their boundless love
and unwavering support.
To my son, Shiva Rudra, whose innocence and light bring new
meaning to life.
And to my friends and family, for their endless encouragement and
companionship.

This book is a tribute to all of you, with love and gratitude.

Contents

Preface

In the depths of emptiness lies untapped potential. This paradox first struck me on Early morning in December, as I sat in my terrace staring at a sky. The emptiness before me was not an absence, but rather an invitation—a space brimming with untapped possibilities, waiting to be transformed into something meaningful.

The void takes many forms in our lives. It might be the silence after losing a job, the uncertainty of starting a new venture, or the blank page confronting a writer. Our instinct is often to fill these spaces immediately, to escape the discomfort of emptiness. But as you'll discover in these pages, the void is not our enemy. It is the canvas upon which we paint our future.

Drawing from psychology, philosophy, art, and contemporary neuroscience, this book offers a radical reframing: emptiness is not a problem to be solved, but a tool to be mastered. Each chapter provides practical frameworks for transforming moments of void into catalysts for action and growth.

To the reader holding this book: you may be experiencing your own void right now. Perhaps you're at a crossroads, feeling stuck, or facing an expanse of uncertainty. Consider this book your companion in transforming that emptiness into possibility. The void is not the end of your story—it's the beginning.

Let us begin this journey together, as we explore how to transmute the raw material of emptiness into the gold of purposeful action.

With gratitude,
Shankar

Acknowledgements

I am deeply grateful to the countless generations of storytellers, teachers, and wisdom-keepers who have preserved and transmitted these tales through the ages. Any oversimplification or deviation from traditional tellings is my responsibility alone, made with the intention of making these precious teachings accessible to contemporary readers.

Remember: These stories are meant to be mirrors in which you might see your own journey reflected. Like all great mythological tales, their true value lies not in historical accuracy but in their power to illuminate the path of self-discovery.

Prologue

Author's Note on Mythological References

In crafting these stories, I have drawn inspiration from India's rich mythological heritage, particularly the great epics Mahabharata and various Puranas. While the core characters and basic frameworks are derived from these ancient texts, I have taken creative liberty in reimagining these tales for modern readers, weaving contemporary relevance into timeless wisdom.

On Adaptation and Interpretation

The stories presented in this book are creative retellings that serve an educational and inspirational purpose. They are not meant to be scholarly translations or strict historical accounts. Rather, they represent a bridge between ancient wisdom and modern understanding, much like how the great oral traditions of India constantly renewed themselves for each generation.

Sources and Inspiration

The core narratives draw from:

The Mahabharata, particularly the Udyoga Parva and Bhishma Parva

Various regional tellings of the epics passed down through generations

Traditional interpretations from different schools of Indian philosophy

Oral traditions preserved by storytellers and spiritual teachers

A Note on Creative Liberty

While characters like Krishna, Arjuna, Karna, and others are revered figures from Indian mythology, their portrayal in these stories has been adapted to illuminate specific modern lessons about personal growth, purpose, and self-discovery. The dialogues, settings, and certain narrative elements have been created to serve the book's educational purpose while maintaining respect for the original sources.

Cultural Context

These stories exist within a vast tapestry of Indian philosophical and spiritual tradition. Terms like 'Svadharma,' 'Karma,' and other Sanskrit concepts have deep, multifaceted meanings that scholars have debated for centuries. The interpretations presented here are meant to be accessible while honoring the depth of these concepts.

Recommended Further Reading

For readers interested in exploring the original sources:

The Mahabharata (Critical Edition by Bhandarkar Oriental Research Institute)

The Bhagavad Gita (Various translations available)

Classical commentaries by scholars like Adi Shankaracharya

Modern academic works on Indian mythology and philosophy

CHAPTER ONE

Introduction: The Nature of the Void

Picture this: It's 11 PM on a Tuesday. Your laptop screen casts a pale glow across your face as you stare at the blank document that should, by now, be a completed project. Instead, you've spent the last three hours scrolling through social media, watching random videos, and responding to non-urgent emails. Your coffee has gone cold, your shoulders are tense, and that familiar feeling of anxiety is creeping up your spine.

You're not alone.

The Paradox of Modern Procrastination

Sarah, a brilliant software engineer, sits in her San Francisco apartment surrounded by three monitors, two tablets, and a smartphone. She has everything she needs to be productive, yet finds herself paralyzed by inaction. Each notification, each new tab opened, becomes another link in the chain of endless distraction.

This is the paradox of our age: We have more productivity tools than ever before, yet struggle more than ever to get things done. Like the ancient Indian tale of the man who searched the world for a precious jewel, only to find it had been hanging around his neck all along, we seek solutions everywhere except where they truly lie – within the spaces between our actions.

Why We Fear Emptiness and Silence

In the bustling streets of ancient Varanasi, a young monk once asked his teacher why people filled their homes with endless possessions. The teacher replied by pouring water into a cup until it overflowed. "Like this cup," he said, "we overflow our lives to avoid seeing what lies beneath."

Today, our overflowing looks different:

- The executive who schedules back-to-back meetings to avoid moments of reflection
- The student who keeps multiple streaming services running in the background while studying
- The writer who checks email every five minutes instead of facing the blank page

We fear empty spaces because, like the still surface of a lake, they reflect back what we've been avoiding: our doubts, our fears, our genuine selves.

The Hidden Potential Within the Void

In the sweltering heat of early 20th century Madras, a young man would often lie on the cool stone floor of the temple, lost in deep meditation. This wasn't your typical temple-goer - this was Srinivasa Ramanujan, whose mind danced with numbers in ways that would later astonish the mathematical world.

While other mathematicians buried themselves in endless calculations, Ramanujan chose a different path. In those still moments on the temple floor, he claimed to experience something extraordinary - a state where mathematical truths weren't laboriously derived, but revealed, as if whispered by the goddess Namagiri herself. His notebooks would later fill with formulas that seemed to emerge from nowhere, patterns so profound that mathematicians are still unraveling their mysteries a century later.

"An equation for me has no meaning," he once said, "unless it expresses a thought of God."

This wasn't mere eccentricity - it echoed an ancient wisdom. In Indian philosophy, there's a concept called 'Shunyata' - the void. But unlike the Western notion of void as a barren nothingness, Shunyata is more like a cosmic womb, a space of infinite potential where all possibilities reside.

Imagine a blank canvas. To the untrained eye, it's empty, worthless. But to an artist, that very emptiness holds every painting that could ever be. Similarly, in Ramanujan's moments of deep silence, his mind wasn't empty - it was touching that same space of infinite potential, where mathematical truths lay waiting to be discovered.

Modern science confirms what Ramanujan and ancient wisdom have long taught us. Research shows that:

- Our most creative insights occur during periods of mental quiet
- Problem-solving abilities improve after periods of undistracted thought
- Memory consolidation happens in the spaces between active learning

- Innovation often emerges from boredom rather than busyness

The Void : A New Approach to an Ancient Truth

The Void Method isn't another productivity system demanding you fill your life with more – more tasks, more tools, more techniques. Instead, it teaches you to find power in space itself, much like the Indian martial art of Kalaripayattu, where the mastery of stillness becomes the foundation of all movement.

The Four Fundamental Shifts: A Journey Through the Void

The day I discovered these four shifts began, ironically, with a complete breakdown of my carefully constructed productivity system. I was sitting in my home office, surrounded by three screens, two phones, and countless productivity apps—all designed to keep me perpetually "on." The notifications were endless, the tasks multiplying, and my mind felt like a browser with too many tabs open. I was drowning in digital noise while accomplishing nothing of substance.

Then, the power went out.

In that sudden darkness, in that unexpected void, something remarkable happened. The silence that I'd been desperately avoiding with notifications and tasks became my teacher. Over the following months, this experience evolved into four fundamental shifts that would transform not just my approach to work, but my entire relationship with emptiness and action.

From Flooding to Flowing

Maria, a creative director I worked with, used to start each day by immediately immersing herself in emails, social media, and news—flooding her mind before she could feel the anxiety of an empty morning. "I thought I was being productive," she told me, "but I was just creating noise." Her breakthrough came when she learned to treat her mornings like a river finding its natural course. Instead of drowning herself in information, she learned to flow with purpose. Now, her most innovative campaigns emerge from those quiet morning hours she once feared.

From Forcing to Allowing

James, a surgeon, approached his practice with military precision until burnout nearly ended his career. His schedule was a fortress of carefully controlled fifteen-minute intervals. "I was at war with time," he reflected. Everything changed when he began studying the natural rhythms of his energy and attention. He discovered that by allowing rather than forcing, by working with his natural cycles rather than against them, he could perform complex procedures with greater skill and less fatigue.

From Fearing to Embracing

The story of Sarah, a novelist, particularly illustrates this shift. For years, she viewed her periods of "writer's block" as the enemy, fighting against them with increasingly desperate techniques. The turning point came when she started treating these vacant periods not as failures but as essential parts of her creative process. "The void," she now says, "is where my stories germinate." Her best-selling novel emerged from what she once would have labeled her worst creative block.

From Fragmenting to Focusing

Alex, a tech entrepreneur, was the master of multitasking—or so he thought. His days were fractured into hundreds of micro-interactions, each one stealing a piece of his attention. His company was successful but stagnant, until a mentor challenged him to experiment with undivided attention. The results were transformative. By focusing deeply on one significant problem at a time, he not only developed his company's breakthrough product but also discovered a sense of fulfillment that had eluded him in his "productive" years.

These shifts aren't just theoretical frameworks—they're gateways to a fundamentally different way of engaging with our work and lives. They teach us that the void isn't an abyss to be feared or filled, but rather a space of infinite potential. When we learn to work with emptiness rather than against it, we don't just become more productive—we become more whole.

The methodology you're about to learn isn't about adding more to your life. It's about transforming your relationship with the space between the doing. It's about discovering that your most powerful moments often come not from adding more, but from learning to dance with emptiness itself.

Think of it as learning to sense the spaces between your thoughts, like a musician who knows that music isn't just in the notes, but in the silences between them. Or like Ramanujan, who discovered that the deepest insights don't come from filling every moment with calculation, but from creating space for infinity to whisper its secrets.

Summary

- We have more productivity tools than ever, yet struggle to get things done.
- We avoid silence and emptiness, fearing the reflection of our doubts and fears.
- Ancient wisdom and modern science suggest that creativity and insight arise from periods of void.
- The void is not nothingness, but a space of infinite potential.
- Focuses on working with emptiness rather than against it.
- Implement four shifts:
- From Flooding to Flowing: Embrace natural rhythms.
- From Forcing to Allowing: Work with your energy cycles.
- From Fearing to Embracing: View "empty" periods as creative spaces.
- From Fragmenting to Focusing: Cultivate undivided attention.

Call to Action:

Start embracing the void. Begin by identifying one small area in your life where you can introduce more space. It could be a 15-minute break in your morning routine, a technology-free evening, or even a few minutes of mindful breathing before starting a task. Observe the impact of this newfound space on your thoughts, feelings, and productivity.

CHAPTER TWO

Confronting the Void

The Dance with Emptiness

"Why do I keep doing this to myself?"

Maya stared at her laptop screen, the cursor blinking mockingly on an empty document. Her deadline was approaching, yet here she was, caught in the familiar dance of avoidance – a tab for emails, another for social media, a third for random articles. Like the rhythm of an endless drum, her fingers tapped restlessly between distractions.

In Indian philosophy, this state has a name: "Alasya" – not mere laziness, but a deep-seated inertia that keeps us bound in patterns of avoidance. It's one of the five kleshas (obstacles) that cloud our true potential.

The Unopened Door

Once in a small, peaceful village, there lived a man named Rishi. Known for his brilliant mind and knack for creativity, Rishi often shared grand dreams of becoming a writer, an artist, and a philosopher. Yet, years passed, and Rishi remained where he was—dreaming, but doing nothing.

One day, a wandering sage came to the village. Hearing of Rishi's talents, the sage visited him and asked, "Why haven't you created anything yet?"

Rishi sighed. "I feel uninspired. There's always tomorrow, and I lack the energy to begin."

The sage looked at him intently. "Do you know what lies beyond that door?" he asked, pointing to the heavy wooden door at the back of Rishi's house.

Rishi hesitated. "It's locked. I've never been curious enough to open it."

The sage smiled. "That door is your Alasya, your inertia. It represents the opportunities you've ignored, the dreams you've postponed. Would you open it if I gave you the key?"

Rishi nodded. The sage handed him a rusty, ancient key and disappeared.

Rishi stared at the door for days. The key sat on his desk, gathering dust. Each time he picked it up, a voice whispered in his mind: **"It's too much effort. What if the door leads to nothing? What if I fail to make sense of what's beyond?"**

Months passed. Rishi finally grew restless, tired of the weight of the unopened door. He picked up the key, unlocked it, and stepped through.

On the other side, he found a lush, beautiful garden filled with rare herbs and fruits. The air was fragrant, and streams of water sparkled under the sun. Rishi realized that all this time, he had been sitting on the edge of abundance but was too paralyzed by inertia to explore it.

The garden became his sanctuary, a place to create his art and write his thoughts. Every day, he thought back to how **Alasya** had chained him to stagnation. He now understood that breaking the inertia required just one step—a step he had postponed for too long.

"Alasya" is not mere laziness—it's a subtle force that feeds on fear and avoidance, keeping us from reaching our true potential. Like the unopened door, it holds us back from the beauty and abundance waiting just beyond our comfort zone. To break free, all it takes is the courage to turn the key.

The Tale of the Five Shadows and the Void

Long ago, in a serene village nestled at the foot of a mighty mountain, there lived a wise monk named Aran. The villagers revered Aran for his wisdom and sought his guidance whenever life felt overwhelming. Despite his peaceful demeanor, Aran was haunted by the Five Shadows, which he referred to as the Five Kleshas—obstacles that clouded the path to enlightenment.

One day, a young seeker named Ishaan came to Aran, desperate to overcome his struggles. "Master, I feel trapped—by fear, doubt, and desires that lead me astray. How can I ever find clarity and peace?"

Aran smiled and gestured toward the mountain. "To answer your question, you must join me on a journey. Together, we will face the Five Shadows and learn how to dissolve them using the Void Method."

The First Shadow: Avidya (Ignorance)

As they began their ascent, the mountain was shrouded in dense fog. Ishaan stumbled on rocks, unable to see the path ahead.

"This is Avidya—the ignorance that blinds us to the truth," Aran said. "We see only the fog and forget that the mountain exists beyond it."

He taught Ishaan the Void Method:

"Close your eyes, stop resisting the fog, and sink into the stillness within. When you embrace the void, the fog loses its power."

Ishaan did as instructed, and as he quieted his mind, the fog lifted, revealing the clear path ahead.

Modern Example:

Maria, a software developer, was overwhelmed by conflicting advice about career progression. Should she learn a new programming language, switch jobs, or focus on her current role? Her ignorance of what truly mattered paralyzed her. Applying the Void Method, she silenced the noise by setting aside her assumptions and sitting quietly with her thoughts. She realized her goal was not about chasing trends but creating meaningful work. The clarity helped her chart a focused path.

The Second Shadow: Asmita (Ego)

Further up, they encountered a narrow ledge. Ishaan froze, overwhelmed by fear of falling.

"This is Asmita—the ego that makes us cling to an image of who we are or must be," said Aran. "Your fear of failure arises from your attachment to that image."

Aran guided him: "Step into the void. Imagine yourself as nothing—no labels, no roles, no boundaries. Just pure awareness."

As Ishaan let go of his ego-driven fear, he found the courage to cross the ledge with ease.

Modern Example:

Ravi, a project manager, hesitated to ask for help on a struggling project because he feared appearing incompetent. His ego clung to the image of being a flawless leader. Using the Void Method, Ravi meditated on detaching from labels like "perfect" or "expert." This freed him to seek advice from his team, who provided valuable insights that turned the project around.

The Third Shadow: Raga (Attachment)

At the next stop, they found a golden fruit tree. Ishaan was mesmerized by its beauty and longed to pick the fruit, but Aran stopped him.

"This is Raga—attachment. Your desire for this fruit binds you, just as other desires chain your mind."

Using the Void Method, Aran instructed Ishaan to focus on the space between himself and the fruit. "Desires are distractions that fill the void. But if you rest in the void, desires dissolve into nothingness."

Ishaan practiced, and the longing disappeared. He smiled, realizing he didn't need the fruit to feel complete.

Modern Example:

Lena, a social media influencer, constantly checked her phone for likes and comments. Her attachment to external validation made her anxious. She tried the Void Method by focusing on the silence behind her need for approval. As she rested in this stillness, her craving faded. She started creating content for its own sake rather than for fleeting recognition.

The Fourth Shadow: Dvesha (Aversion)

Soon, they faced a steep slope covered in thorns. Ishaan hesitated, repelled by the pain it might bring.

"This is Dvesha—aversion. It's the flip side of attachment, where we resist what we dislike or fear."

Aran guided him to the Void Method again. "Imagine the thorns are part of the void—neither good nor bad, just part of the whole. When you stop resisting, you can walk through them freely."

To his surprise, Ishaan crossed the slope with minimal pain, realizing it was his resistance that made the thorns seem sharper.

Modern Example:

Mark, a sales executive, dreaded cold-calling clients. His aversion made every call feel like a mountain. Practicing the Void Method, Mark visualized the calls as neutral events, stripping them of emotional weight. This mindset shift reduced his anxiety, and he approached each call with calmness and efficiency.

The Fifth Shadow: Abhinivesha (Fear of Death)

Finally, they reached the peak, but a deep chasm separated them from the summit. Ishaan stepped back, terrified of falling into the abyss.

"This is Abhinivesha—the fear of death, the ultimate attachment to life as we know it," Aran said.

Aran instructed Ishaan to sit at the edge and look into the chasm. "The void is nothingness, but it is also infinite potential. Embrace the void, and you'll see that death is not the end—it's just a part of the flow."

As Ishaan meditated, he felt his fear dissolve into peace. He stepped across the chasm, feeling lighter than ever before.

Modern Example:

Emma, a terminally ill patient, struggled with the fear of dying. Guided by the Void Method, she meditated on the concept of nothingness as a space for infinite possibilities. This practice helped her transcend her fear, allowing her to spend her final days in peace, appreciating the beauty of the present moment.

As Ishaan reached the summit, he felt a profound stillness within. The Five Shadows no longer bound him. Aran smiled and said, "The void is not emptiness but a space where all things are possible. By embracing it, you've dissolved the obstacles that cloud the path to clarity and peace."

The Modern Chakravyuha

Picture a young warrior prince, Abhimanyu, standing before a swirling military formation known as the Chakravyuha. The formation moved like a living thing, soldiers shifting in intricate patterns, creating a maze that had claimed countless lives. Abhimanyu knew how to enter – he had learned this while still in his mother's womb. But the crucial knowledge of how to exit was missing, lost in an interrupted conversation when his pregnant mother fell asleep.

Like Abhimanyu, we modern warriors find ourselves trapped in our own Chakravyuha – a maze far more subtle and seductive than any military formation. Instead of soldiers, we face an army of digital distractions, each one beckoning with promises of momentary escape.

Maya's screen glows with familiar patterns. A notification pops up – just a quick check won't hurt. Her finger moves instinctively, muscle memory performing the ancient dance of avoidance in modern form. One click leads to another, each promising to be the last, each drawing her deeper into the formation.

The statistics tell a story as haunting as any ancient epic:

- Our hands touch our phones 2,617 times each day – modern mantras of distraction
- Every 18 minutes, a notification pierces our concentration like an arrow
- Our attention span, once a robust 12 seconds, has dwindled to 8 – faster than a goldfish's
- Nearly half our online time vanishes into the void of procrastination

The parallels to Abhimanyu's tale grow stronger:

The Entry Point

Like the prince confidently breaching the first layer of the formation, we begin with a moment of discomfort or uncertainty. The deadline looms, the blank page stares, and we reach for our phone. The first scroll brings relief – we're in.

The Spiral

Abhimanyu fought deeper into the formation, each layer drawing him further from safety. We too spiral inward – one video leads to another, one article suggests three more, each click pulling us deeper into the maze. Time becomes fluid, minutes bleeding into hours.

The Trapped State

The young warrior realized too late he was trapped, surrounded by forces he couldn't overcome. We share his fate in digital form, knowing we should stop, feeling the anxiety build, yet unable to break free. The ancient texts call this state "Vikshepa" – the scattered mind, lost in its own maze.

Our modern Chakravyuha is engineered with a precision that would make ancient strategists envious:

- Infinite scrolling feeds that move like the rotating layers of the original formation
- Notifications that trigger dopamine releases, the brain's own warrior rushing to battle
- Algorithms that learn our weaknesses, adapting like a living opponent
- Content that plays on our deepest insecurities, holding us in place with invisible chains

The Wisdom of Emptiness

In the Yoga Sutras, Patanjali speaks of "Chitta Vritti Nirodha" – the cessation of mental fluctuations. This state, similar to Musashi's "no-mind," emerges not from adding more, but from learning to be with less.

Consider this story:

A young musician approached his guru, complaining about his inability to compose. The guru took him to a busy street corner in Varanasi and asked him to listen to all the sounds – the vendors shouting, bells ringing, vehicles honking.

"Now," said the guru, "listen to the silence between these sounds."

The musician thought this impossible at first, but as he practiced, he began to notice the tiny spaces between sounds. His music transformed as he learned to appreciate these intervals as much as the notes themselves.

The Journey Through the Void

Maya sat in her apartment, the morning light painting shadows across her meditation cushion. The same cushion that had gathered dust for months now called to her like an old friend. Her phone lay face-down on her desk – a small act of rebellion against its usual gravitational pull.

She remembered the words of her grandfather, a meditation teacher in Bangalore: "Even the mightiest ocean begins with a single drop." Today, she would start with a drop.

The Four Gateways: Ancient Practices for the Modern Mind

The Sacred Pause: First Gateway

Like a master swordsman learning to still their blade between strikes, Maya began with the simplest of practices – the sacred pause. Before each reflexive reach for her phone, she would take one conscious breath.

"Just three times a day," she promised herself. "Three moments of sanity."

The first day, she caught herself mid-reach, her hand hovering over her phone like a hummingbird. One breath. The urge to check notifications buzzed through her body like electricity. Another breath. Something shifted – subtle but unmistakable. The space between impulse and action widened, just a fraction.

The Emptiness Timer: Second Gateway

"Two minutes?" Maya laughed when she first heard the instruction. "I spend hours on social media, and you want me to sit for two minutes?"

But as she sat there, timer ticking away, those two minutes stretched like an eternity. Her thoughts raced like wild horses – deadlines, emails, that embarrassing thing she said three years ago. Yet something strange happened. Like clouds passing across the sky, she began to notice gaps between the thoughts.

Digital Sandhya - The Twilight Practice: Third Gateway

In ancient India, Sandhya marked the sacred transition times – dawn, noon, and dusk. Maya created her own modern Sandhyas, small ceremonies between activities. Five minutes of silence before opening her laptop. A moment of stillness before each Zoom call.

Her coworkers noticed the difference. "You seem... present," one said during a meeting. Maya smiled, thinking of the small ritual she had performed just moments before – five breaths, eyes closed, letting the previous meeting's energy dissolve like morning mist.

The Witness Practice: Fourth Gateway

This was the hardest gateway – facing the void itself. When procrastination struck, instead of running, she would pause. Name three sensations: tight chest, sweaty palms, shallow breath. Notice the fear beneath the avoidance: fear of imperfection, fear of judgment, fear of the blank page.

Thirty seconds. She would stay for thirty seconds, like a warrior learning to stand her ground.

Maya's Journey Through the Void

What began as simple exercises evolved into a profound transformation. Like a scientist documenting a new discovery, Maya tracked her journey through the unknown:

Week 1: First Steps into the Void

The numbers startled her – 89 phone checks in a single day. Each check marked on her "distraction diary" like breadcrumbs leading back through a maze. Peak procrastination times emerged: 10:30 AM, just before starting difficult tasks. 3:00 PM, when energy dipped. 11:00 PM, when the day's unfinished business loomed large.

"Know your enemy," her grandfather used to say. But was this enemy really an ally in disguise?

Week 2: Dancing with Resistance

The urges came like waves. During one focused work session, her hands actually trembled with the desire to check social media. Physical sensations arose – a knot in her stomach, a tightness in her throat.

But beneath these symptoms, she discovered something unexpected: a deep fear of imperfection. Each moment of discomfort became a tiny window into her own patterns.

Week 3: Glimpses of Freedom

Something shifted in the third week. During her morning Sandhya practice, Maya experienced a moment of pure clarity – like a lake becoming still enough to reflect the sky perfectly. These moments began appearing during work as well, islands of natural focus in the sea of distraction.

She wrote in her journal: "The void isn't empty – it's pregnant with possibility."

Week 4: The New Dance

By the fourth week, Maya had developed a different relationship with space and time. Like a musician who appreciates the silence between notes, she found herself valuing the pauses between activities. Her days took on a natural rhythm – periods of intense focus balanced with conscious breaks.

Her grandfather's voice echoed in her memory: "In Sanskrit, we call the smallest unit of time 'Kshana' – a moment so brief it contains the seed of transformation." Maya understood now. Each conscious pause, each tiny victory over distraction, was a Kshana – a moment pregnant with possibility.

The Path Ahead

The ancient text Yoga Vasistha tells us: "What we run from pursues us, what we face transforms us." Your procrastination isn't your enemy – it's a teacher waiting to reveal profound truths about your patterns, fears, and untapped potential.

Consider these words from an ancient text: "The warrior who knows when to be still becomes invincible." Our journey begins not with fighting our distractions, but with learning to observe them with the patience of a master strategist.

Your Practice This Week:

1. Choose one exercise from above
2. Start with just 3 minutes daily
3. Note what arises when you pause
4. Remember: discomfort is not failure

The void isn't empty – it's where everything begins. Like Abhimanyu's story, your journey through the modern Chakravyuha may seem daunting. But unlike him, you have the wisdom of both ancient traditions and modern understanding to guide you. Are you ready to take your first conscious step into it?

Summary

- We live in an age of unprecedented productivity tools, yet struggle to achieve our goals due to constant distractions. This text explores the concept of "Alasya" – an inner inertia that leads to avoidance and inaction.
- Drawing from ancient Indian philosophy, the text introduces the Five Kleshas (obstacles): Ignorance, Ego, Attachment, Aversion, and Fear of Death. These shadows cloud our judgment and hinder our progress.
- Based on ancient wisdom and modern insights, the Void Method emphasizes the importance of embracing

stillness and finding power in the spaces between our actions. It involves four key shifts:

- Cultivating conscious pauses throughout the day.
- Scheduling short periods of deliberate stillness.
- Creating sacred transitions between activities.
- Observing thoughts and emotions without judgment.
- The Modern Chakravyuha: The text draws a parallel between modern distractions (social media, notifications) and the ancient Indian military formation, the Chakravyuha. This highlights how digital distractions can trap us in a cycle of avoidance.

Call to Action:

The text encourages readers to:

- Acknowledge the presence of "Alasya" in their own lives.
- Choose one exercise from the Void Method and practice it consistently for at least 3 minutes daily.
- Observe their thoughts and emotions during these exercises without judgment.
- Remember that discomfort is not failure.
- Recognize that the void is not empty, but a space of potential.

CHAPTER THREE

The Power of Subtraction: Where Less Becomes Everything

The old monk's laughter echoed through the ancient temple halls, bouncing off stone walls that had stood witness to centuries of wisdom. "You remind me of myself," he said to the young tech executive who sat before him, her laptop balanced precariously on crossed legs. "Always trying to add more, when the secret lies in taking away."

Sarah shifted uncomfortably on the meditation cushion, her phone buzzing for the fifteenth time that hour. She had flown halfway across the world seeking answers to her burnout, only to find this enigmatic monk who seemed more interested in the space between things than the things themselves.

"Tell me," he continued, his eyes twinkling with ancient mischief, "what do you see in this temple?"

Sarah glanced around, her corporate-trained eyes automatically cataloging and categorizing. "Well, there's the altar, the statues, the—"

"No," he interrupted gently. "What do you *really* see?"

And then it hit her. What made the temple extraordinary wasn't what was there—it was what wasn't. Between each statue stretched vast spaces of emptiness. Between each pillar, silence. Between each thought, a breath of possibility.

"Space," she whispered. "I see space."

The monk nodded, pleased. "Now look at your life."

Sarah didn't need to look far. Her phone buzzed again, a perfect metaphor for her cluttered existence. Sixty-five apps competing for attention. Ten thousand photos she never looked at. Three hundred browser tabs she'd never read. Her life had become a temple to excess, every corner stuffed with digital offerings to the gods of More.

"But how?" she asked. "How do I even begin to empty my cup when it's not just full—it's overflowing?"

The monk rose and walked to a nearby shelf, returning with a simple clay cup and a pot of tea. Without a word, he began to pour. The tea rose to the brim, then spilled over, creating a small puddle on the ancient stone floor.

"Master, the cup is full!" Sarah exclaimed, tech-executive efficiency kicking in.

His smile deepened. "Exactly. Like this cup, your life cannot receive anything new until you create space for it. Let me share with you the three temples of space—physical, digital, and mental. Each one, when properly emptied, becomes not an absence, but a presence."

Over the next three weeks, Sarah embarked on what she later called her "Subtraction Pilgrimage." Week one began with her desk—her modern-day altar. She removed everything, down to the last paperclip. The empty surface felt both terrifying and thrilling, like standing on the edge of a cliff.

Week two tackled her digital life. "Think of your phone as a zen garden," the monk suggested. "Each app should be like a carefully placed stone—purposeful, meaningful, necessary." She deleted 80% of her apps, feeling a strange mixture of loss and liberation with each tap.

The third week ventured into the most cluttered temple of all—her mind. Through morning pages and what the monk called "the sacred no," she began to clear the mental static that had become her constant companion.

The transformation wasn't immediate or easy. There were moments of panic, of reaching for deleted apps like phantom limbs. But slowly, like sun breaking through clouds, clarity emerged.

A month later, Sarah sat in the same temple, on the same cushion. But everything felt different. Her phone lay silent in her bag. Her laptop remained closed. Her mind, for the first time in years, felt spacious enough to hear her own thoughts.

"You see," the monk said, pouring tea into her now-empty cup, "the power of subtraction isn't in what you remove—it's in what you reveal. Like the space between stars that allows us to see constellations, or the silence between notes that creates music."

Sarah watched the steam rise from her cup, dancing in the empty air. "I think I finally understand," she said. "It's not about having nothing. It's about having the right things, with enough space between them to breathe."

The monk nodded, pleased. "And now that you have space, what will you do with it?"

Sarah closed her eyes, feeling the vast potential of emptiness spreading before her like an unwritten page. For the first time in years, she felt not the urge to fill it, but to let it speak.

In the distance, a temple bell rang, its sound carried by the very emptiness that made its music possible.

The King's Journey of Subtraction:

King Ashoka, one of India's most powerful rulers, experienced a profound shift in his life that mirrors the very journey Sarah was on. Ashoka was initially known for his ruthless conquests and wars, particularly during his brutal campaign to expand his empire, most famously during the Kalinga War. After the victory, Ashoka was confronted with the unimaginable devastation caused by the war—the countless lives lost, the suffering, and the devastation of his own people. This moment of witnessing the horrors of war led him to a deep realization.

The story goes that, after the battle, Ashoka wandered the battlefield, seeing the pain and destruction his ambition had caused. The sight of suffering overwhelmed him, and he found himself grappling with a profound sense of emptiness. It was in this moment of intense emotional turmoil that Ashoka made a drastic decision—he renounced the ways of conquest, and instead turned toward a path of peace and spiritual awakening. He chose to embrace Buddhism, a philosophy that emphasized the renunciation of violence, greed, and ego.

Ashoka's decision to abandon his former life of conquest was his own version of subtraction. He could have continued expanding his empire, amassing more power and wealth, but he chose a different path—one of self-restraint and inner peace. He began to reduce the suffering he had caused, focusing on welfare, religious tolerance, and peace. His transformation was not about gaining more, but about eliminating the distractions and desires that led him down a destructive path.

Like the monk's lesson of creating space for what truly matters, Ashoka's life shifted from an empire built on conquest to one founded on dharma (righteousness). In his later years, he became known as Ashoka the Great, not for the battles he fought, but for the peace he fostered, his commitment to nonviolence, and his dedication to serving the welfare of his people. His famous Edicts of Ashoka, inscribed on pillars across the subcontinent, speak of compassion, tolerance, and the importance of spiritual and social harmony—principles that emerged only after he had subtracted the pursuit of material glory and conquest from his life.

In Sarah's story, Ashoka's transformation can serve as a powerful reminder that sometimes, the most meaningful shift in life comes not from acquiring more, but from letting go of the destructive habits and desires that keep us from our true purpose. Ashoka's story of renunciation and finding inner peace after his greatest victory highlights how subtraction can lead to profound growth, both personally and spiritually.

Just as Ashoka reduced his focus on external power and embraced internal peace, Sarah could reflect on what parts of her life—her constant pursuit of more, her need for validation through digital presence, or her unrelenting drive for success—are causing unnecessary suffering or distraction. Like Ashoka, the goal isn't to achieve more; it's to subtract the things that no longer serve her well-being and make space for what truly matters.

Ashoka's story would serve as a poignant example for Sarah—and anyone on a journey of self-discovery—showing that the true strength lies not in conquest, but in the power of renunciation and creating space for peace.

Your Journey Begins:

1. Look around your space right now. What could you remove to let your life's music play more clearly?
2. Choose one temple—physical, digital, or mental—to begin your own subtraction pilgrimage.
3. Remember: the goal isn't emptiness for emptiness's sake, but space for what truly matters.

Are you ready to discover the power of less?

Summary

- In a world of constant stimulation and the pursuit of "more," true fulfillment often lies in subtraction.
- The text highlights the importance of creating space in three key areas:
- Physical: Decluttering physical spaces to reduce mental clutter.
- Digital: Curating digital experiences by minimizing distractions and focusing on essential apps.
- Mental: Cultivating mental stillness through practices like meditation and mindfulness.
- Inspired by the story of King Ashoka, the text emphasizes that true progress often comes from subtracting unnecessary pursuits and focusing on what

truly matters.

- Emptying the cup allows for new possibilities and deeper connections with oneself and the world.

Call to Action:

- Identify areas in your physical, digital, and mental life where you can create more space.
- Choose one area to focus on and take a small, concrete step towards subtraction.
- Embrace the discomfort that may arise as you let go of old habits and attachments.
- Remember that the goal is not to become empty, but to create space for what truly matters.

CHAPTER FOUR

Action in the Present: The Dance of Imperfect Progress

The cursor blinked mockingly on Sarah's screen, a digital metronome counting the beats of her hesitation. Outside her window, the first rays of dawn painted Mumbai's skyline in shades of gold, marking the third straight night she'd spent tweaking the same presentation. Each slide was a masterpiece of precision, yet she couldn't bring herself to call it complete.

"Just one more adjustment," she whispered, the same words she'd repeated like a mantra for the past seventy-two hours. Her coffee had gone cold, again.

A gentle knock interrupted her spiral of perfectionism. It was Raj, the elderly office custodian, whose wisdom had a habit of appearing exactly when needed.

"You remind me of the story of the master archer," he said, setting down a fresh cup of chai on her desk. "Would you like to hear it?"

Sarah nodded, grateful for any distraction from the presentation that had become her gilded cage.

"There was once an archer named Arjuna," Raj began, his voice carrying the weight of ancient wisdom. "His guru gave him a peculiar challenge: to perfect his art in complete darkness. 'Impossible!' Arjuna protested. 'How can I hit what I cannot see perfectly?'"

Raj smiled knowingly at Sarah's screen. "Sound familiar?"

Sarah glanced at her presentation—all forty-seven meticulously crafted slides. "But this needs to be perfect. The board meeting—"

"Ah," Raj interrupted, "but did you know that according to our ancient texts, even the universe itself emerged from chaos? Creation is messy, yet look at the beauty it produced." He gestured toward the sunrise painting the sky outside.

"But how did Arjuna do it?" Sarah asked, suddenly more interested in the ancient archer than her modern predicament.

"He began," Raj said simply. "In the darkness, he drew his bow again and again. Each arrow taught him something—the whisper of the wind, the tension in the string, the weight of his own doubt. Through action, not perfection, he became legendary."

Sarah looked at her presentation with new eyes. "So you're saying I should just... start? Even if it's not perfect?"

Raj pulled out a small notebook from his pocket. "Let me show you something. Every day, I write down one small victory. Today's was fixing the stubborn coffee machine on the third floor. Yesterday's was helping a lost delivery person find their way. None of these actions were perfect, but they were complete."

He placed the notebook on her desk. "May I?" he asked, reaching for her laptop. With a few quick clicks, he divided her presentation into five clear sections. "Now, choose one section—just one—and give yourself five minutes to work on it. Not perfect, just progress."

"Five minutes?" Sarah laughed. "What can I possibly accomplish in five minutes?"

"More than you'll accomplish in five hours of hesitation," Raj winked. "It's what we call 'aarambh'—the sacred art of beginning."

Over the next four days, Sarah embarked on what she later called her "Imperfect Revolution." Following Raj's wisdom, she:

Day 1: Committed to five-minute focused sessions, surprised to find herself naturally working longer

Day 2: Broke down each section into 25-minute tasks, celebrating each small completion

Day 3: Kept a "Progress Journal," documenting insights and unexpected breakthroughs

Day 4: Found herself flowing between tasks with newfound ease, no longer haunted by the ghost of perfection

Like a potter at the wheel, she learned to let her work take shape through action rather than endless planning. Each "imperfect" step revealed new possibilities she couldn't have seen from the paralysis of perfectionism.

The morning of her board presentation arrived. As Sarah stood before the executives, she felt different. Her presentation wasn't perfect—she could still see tiny adjustments she could make—but it was powerful, authentic, and most importantly, complete.

After receiving a standing ovation, she found Raj cleaning the conference room.

"You knew, didn't you?" she asked. "That it was never about the presentation being perfect?"

He smiled, wiping down the table with careful, practiced movements. "In our tradition, we say 'karma yoga'—the yoga of action. Every task, however small, is a step toward something greater. Your presentation wasn't just about slides and data; it was about breaking free from the chains of perfectionism."

Sarah pulled out her own notebook—a habit she'd picked up from Raj—and wrote: "Today's victory: Embraced imperfect action. Result: Perfect breakthrough."

The Lesson of Eklavya's Thumb

In the dense forests of ancient India, there lived a young tribal boy named Eklavya who dreamed of becoming the greatest archer in the world. Every day, he would watch from afar as the legendary guru Dronacharya taught archery to the Pandava and Kaurava princes. When Dronacharya refused to teach him due to his low birth, Eklavya did something remarkable – he built a clay statue of Dronacharya, declared it his guru, and began his practice.

In the shadow of ancient trees, Eklavya trained with unmatched dedication. His pursuit of perfection was so intense that he would practice in complete darkness, learning to shoot arrows guided by sound alone. He would practice until his fingers bled, then practice more. When birds disturbed his concentration, he developed the ability to shoot multiple arrows simultaneously, so precise that he could silence a barking dog without harming it.

One day, Arjuna, the greatest among Dronacharya's students, discovered Eklavya's abilities. Troubled that someone had surpassed him, Arjuna approached Dronacharya. The guru, bound by his promise to make Arjuna the world's greatest archer, visited Eklavya.

Seeing Eklavya's clay statue of himself, Dronacharya asked, "If you consider me your guru, will you give me my guru-dakshina (teacher's fee)?"

"Anything, my lord," Eklavya replied without hesitation.

"Give me your right thumb."

Without a moment's pause, Eklavya drew his knife and cut off his thumb, placing it at the clay statue's feet. With this act, he lost his ability to shoot arrows with his former perfection.

But here's where the story takes an unexpected turn, one often forgotten in retellings. Eklavya did not abandon archery. Instead, he learned to shoot differently, developing new techniques that didn't require a thumb. His imperfection became his innovation. He discovered that there were many ways to be an archer, each with its own beauty and effectiveness.

Years later, when asked about his greatest achievement, Eklavya didn't speak of his perfect shots or his legendary speed. Instead, he said, "My greatest victory was learning that perfection isn't about being flawless – it's about being adaptable."

The Dance of Nataraj

In the courts of Mount Kailash, shiva prepared to perform the Tandava, But among them sat Tandu, Shiva's dance instructor, lost in contemplation of his own imperfection.

Tandu had spent millennia perfecting every mudra (hand gesture), every movement, every rhythm of the sacred dance. Yet he felt unworthy to be called Shiva's teacher, for how could a mortal's dance ever achieve divine perfection?

Seeing his teacher's distress, Shiva paused before beginning his dance. "Why do you doubt yourself, my friend?"

Tandu replied, "I have spent lifetimes pursuing the perfect dance, yet each movement I create feels inadequate . Perhaps I should stop teaching altogether."

Shiva smiled and began to dance. But instead of the traditional Tandava, he incorporated what others might call "mistakes" – movements that broke with classical form, rhythms that defied conventional patterns. Yet somehow, these imperfections made the dance more mesmerizing, more alive.

After the dance, Shiva turned to his bewildered teacher. "Did you see any imperfection in my dance?"

"It was different from the classical form," Tandu admitted, "but it was... perfect in its own way."

"Exactly," Shiva replied. "I am called Nataraj – the lord of dance – not because I execute every movement flawlessly, but because I understand that the universe itself is an improvised dance. Creation isn't about achieving perfection; it's about embracing the divine play of existence."

Tandu suddenly understood. His years of teaching hadn't been about achieving perfect form – they had been about understanding the essence of movement itself. His perceived imperfections weren't flaws but variations in the cosmic dance.

From that day forward, Tandu's dance academy changed. Instead of demanding rigid perfection, he taught his students to find their own rhythm within the classical framework. His students learned that true mastery wasn't about performing without errors, but about dancing with such authenticity that even mistakes became beautiful.

As centuries passed, Tandu's school became known not for producing the most technically perfect dancers, but for nurturing artists who could make the hearts of gods and mortals dance with them. His greatest lesson became: "Dance not for perfection, but for the joy of being part of the cosmic choreography."

Your Journey Begins:

1. What masterpiece are you holding hostage to perfectionism?
2. Can you give it the gift of five minutes today?
3. What small victory will you celebrate first?

Remember: Like the ancient archer learning to shoot in darkness, your path to mastery begins not with perfect conditions, but with the courage to begin.

Are you ready to take your first imperfect step?

Summary:

- The text highlights how the pursuit of perfection can lead to procrastination and inaction, hindering progress.
- The stories of Arjuna, Eklavya, and Tandu emphasize the importance of taking action, even if it's imperfect, to achieve progress and learn from the process.
- The concept of "aarambh" (the sacred art of beginning) is introduced as a key to overcoming the fear of imperfection.
- The text suggests that true creativity and growth often arise from embracing the "messiness" of the creative

process.
- The focus shifts from achieving a predetermined goal to finding joy and fulfillment in the process of creation and learning.

Core Idea:

The core idea of the text is that true progress and fulfillment are not achieved through the pursuit of perfection, but through embracing imperfect action and finding joy in the journey. By focusing on taking small steps, learning from mistakes, and celebrating each accomplishment, individuals can break free from the paralysis of perfectionism and unlock their true potential.

Call to Action:

The text encourages readers to:

- Identify an area in their life where they are struggling with perfectionism.
- Take a small, imperfect step towards their goal.
- Embrace the "messiness" of the process and learn from their mistakes.
- Celebrate small victories and find joy in the journey.

CHAPTER FIVE

Finding Purpose in Emptiness

Maya sat in her local park, watching children play with complete absorption in their games. Their natural sense of purpose struck her. When had she last felt that level of engagement with her work? Like many of us, she had mastered the mechanics of productivity but lost touch with its meaning.

In the Upanishads, there's a beautiful concept called "Svadharma" – your unique purpose or personal truth. Finding it requires not adding more to your life, but stripping away what isn't authentically yours.

The autumn breeze carried the sound of children's laughter as Maya closed her laptop, the quarterly reports blurring into meaningless numbers. Twenty years into her career, she had everything she'd been told to want: the corner office, the impressive title, the comfortable salary. Yet something felt hollow, like an ornate frame around an empty canvas.

"Stuck again?" A familiar voice interrupted her thoughts. It was Dev, the elderly yoga instructor who taught morning classes in the park. His eyes carried the kind of wisdom that comes from living life rather than just reading about it.

"How did you know?" Maya asked, making space for him on the bench.

Dev smiled, watching the children at play. "You have the same look I once had – successful on the outside, searching on the inside." He pulled out a worn journal from his bag. "Let me share a story from my own journey."

Opening the journal, he revealed a simple circle drawn on the page, divided into four quadrants. "In our tradition, we speak of the four Purusharthas – the four aims of life. Think of them as compass points on your journey to purpose."

Maya leaned in, intrigued. "Tell me more."

"First, there's Dharma – your unique purpose. Think of it as your personal North Star. Then Artha – prosperity, but not just money. Kama – not just pleasure, but deep satisfaction. And finally, Moksha – liberation from all that isn't truly you."

He pointed to the playing children. "Watch them. They naturally express their Svadharma – their authentic nature. We adults? We've buried ours under layers of 'should' and 'must.'"

Over the next four weeks, Dev became Maya's guide on what she later called her "Purpose Pilgrimage." Each week brought a new revelation:

Week 1: The Mountain Peak

"Imagine you're at the end of your life," Dev suggested during their morning walks. "What three achievements would make you feel your life was well-lived?"

Maya's answers surprised her. None involved titles or promotions. Instead, she wrote:

- Creating spaces where people feel seen and heard
- Building bridges between different worlds and perspectives
- Leaving a legacy of wisdom for future generations

"Interesting," Dev noted. "Your soul speaks in patterns. Listen carefully."

Week 2: The Three Gates

Dev taught Maya an ancient decision-making filter: "Before taking any action, ask yourself: Is it true to me? Is it beneficial? Is it timely?"

Applying these questions to her work projects was like turning on a light in a dusty room. Some tasks that seemed important failed the authenticity test. Others she'd been postponing suddenly felt urgent when viewed through this lens.

Week 3: The Purpose Prototype

"Choose one core value," Dev challenged her. "Live it fully for just one day. See what changes."

Maya chose 'wisdom-sharing.' She transformed her dreaded quarterly review into a learning session for her team, sharing not just numbers but insights. The energy in the room shifted tangibly. For the first time in years, she left work feeling energized rather than drained.

Week 4: The Integration

By the final week,

Maya had developed what she called her "Purpose Pyramid":

- At the base: Necessary tasks, but reframed through purpose
- In the middle: Projects that sparked genuine engagement
- At the top: Initiatives that expressed her highest values

One morning, she arrived at the park to find Dev sitting with a group of business professionals, sharing ancient wisdom in modern terms. "Your Svadharma," she observed with a smile.

"Indeed," he replied. "When you strip away what isn't yours, what remains is your gift to the world. Speaking of which..." He nodded toward her laptop bag.

Maya pulled out her resignation letter – not from her job, but from the parts of it that didn't align with her purpose. She had renegotiated her role to focus on mentoring and strategic wisdom-sharing, her natural strengths.

"The children taught us well," Dev said, watching a young girl completely absorbed in building a sandcastle. "Purpose isn't something you find..."

"It's something you uncover," Maya finished, feeling the truth of it in her bones.

The Choice of Karna

In the great halls of Hastinapura, Karna stood before Krishna, his heart heavy with an impossible choice. The divine messenger had just revealed to him a truth that shattered his world: he was not the son of a charioteer, but the firstborn of Kunti, making him the eldest of the Pandavas – his sworn enemies.

"You can claim your true identity," Krishna said softly. "Take your rightful place among the Pandavas. The kingdom would be yours to rule, as is your birthright."

Karna's hands trembled, but his voice remained steady. "And what of my foster father, who raised me with love despite our poverty? What of Duryodhana, who gave me respect and friendship when others scorned me for my supposed low birth?"

Krishna watched him intently. "Is it not your Svadharma to be who you truly are – a prince, a leader, a Pandava?"

Karna smiled sadly. "But who am I truly, Krishna? The accident of my birth makes me a Pandava, but every choice I've made, every loyalty I've built, every promise I've kept – these make me who I am. Is that not a truer Svadharma than the one granted by birth?"

Standing by the window, watching the sun set over the kingdom he could have ruled, Karna made his choice. "My Svadharma is not to be a king by birth, but to be a friend in truth. I choose loyalty over power, gratitude over gain."

As history would later record, Karna's decision led to his ultimate sacrifice in the great war. Yet, in choosing to honor his inner truth over external expectations, he achieved something greater than a kingdom – he fulfilled his Svadharma as the embodiment of unwavering loyalty and personal truth.

Years later, when scholars debated Karna's choice, Krishna would say, "He could have had a kingdom, but he chose instead to rule over something far greater – his own heart."

The Dance of Abhimanyu

Young Abhimanyu sat beneath the ancient banyan tree, tears of frustration streaming down his face. His father, the great Arjuna, had just departed for a thirteen-year exile, leaving behind a son desperate to prove himself worthy of his father's legacy.

An old wandering minstrel, watching the boy's distress, approached with a veena in his hands. "Why do you weep, young warrior?"

"I am Abhimanyu, son of Arjuna," the boy declared proudly through his tears. "But how can I fulfill my Svadharma as a great warrior like my father when he's not here to teach me?"

The minstrel sat beside him, tuning his veena. "Let me tell you a secret about the honeybee," he said, playing a gentle melody. "From the moment it's born, it knows how to dance."

"But I'm not a honeybee," Abhimanyu protested. "I'm a warrior who doesn't even know the complete art of warfare!"

"Ah, but like the bee, you carry your truth within you," the minstrel replied. "Your father Arjuna is known for learning every military formation, but do you know why he succeeded? Not because he copied others, but because he found his own dance in battle."

Over the next several days, the minstrel taught Abhimanyu through stories and songs, each one revealing a different aspect of Svadharma. He spoke of warriors who succeeded not by following prescribed paths, but by discovering their unique strengths.

"Your father's greatest skill isn't archery," the minstrel revealed. "It's his ability to be fully present in whatever he does. That's his true Svadharma – and you have that same gift."

Understanding dawned on Abhimanyu. He began to train differently, not trying to replicate his father's techniques exactly, but finding his own rhythm in battle. He learned to combine his natural agility with innovative thinking, developing a style uniquely his own.

Years later, in the great battle of Kurukshetra, Abhimanyu would face his greatest test – the Chakravyuha, a complex military formation. Though he hadn't learned its complete solution, his unique approach – born from understanding his true nature – allowed him to penetrate the formation in ways that even seasoned warriors couldn't predict.

Though history remembers his tragic end in that battle, it also celebrates how a young warrior found his Svadharma not in copying his famous father, but in being authentically himself. As the bards would sing: "He danced his own dance in the cosmic play, and for a moment, made the gods themselves pause to watch."

The minstrel, who was none other than Krishna in disguise, would later tell Arjuna, "Your son's greatest victory wasn't in following your path – it was in finding his own."

Your Journey Begins:

1. What layers of "should" are hiding your authentic purpose?
2. Which of the four Purusharthas needs your attention now?
3. What would you do today if you could act from pure authenticity?

Remember: Like the children in the park, your deepest purpose isn't waiting to be created – it's waiting to be remembered.

Are you ready to uncover your Svadharma?

Summary:

- Your Unique Purpose: The text explores the concept of Svadharma – your unique purpose or personal truth. It emphasizes that finding your Svadharma involves identifying and aligning with your authentic self.
- The text introduces the four aims of life: Dharma (purpose), Artha (prosperity), Kama (fulfillment), and Moksha (liberation). These provide a framework for understanding and aligning with one's Svadharma.
- Finding your Svadharma requires stripping away the layers of societal expectations, external pressures, and inauthentic pursuits that obscure your true nature.
- The Stories of Maya, Ashoka, Karna, and Abhimanyu: These stories illustrate how individuals can discover and live in alignment with their Svadharma.

Core Idea:

The core idea of the text is that true fulfillment comes from living in alignment with your Svadharma – your unique purpose. This involves a process of self-discovery that requires you to:

- Identify your true values and passions.
- Strip away the layers of societal expectations and inauthentic pursuits.
- Embrace your unique strengths and weaknesses.
- Focus on living a life that is meaningful and authentic to you.

Call to Action:

The text encourages readers to:

- Reflect on their own lives and identify areas where they may be living out of alignment with their Svadharma.
- Explore the four Purusharthas and consider how they apply to their own lives.
- Engage in introspection and self-reflection to uncover their true values and passions.
- Take small steps towards living a life that is more authentic and aligned with their Svadharma.

CHAPTER SIX

Detachment and Flow: Dancing with the Present

The cursor blinked rhythmically on Maya's screen, mocking her indecision. Draft number eight of the same email sat before her, each word feeling more forced than the last. Her mind raced with an endless stream of "what-ifs" – what the ancient texts called "chitta vritti," the whirlpool of thoughts that drowns our natural clarity.

"Just send it," she whispered to herself, but her finger remained frozen above the mouse. The modern corporate warrior, paralyzed by her own thoughts.

"You know," came a gentle voice, "there's a reason why Lord Shiva is called Nataraja – the lord of the dance."

Maya looked up to find her elderly neighbor, Arun, a retired dance teacher, standing at her home office doorway. She had forgotten he was coming over for their weekly chai session. His presence was always a reminder of a different way of being – more flowing, less forced.

"What do you mean?" Maya asked, grateful for any distraction from her email purgatory.

Arun settled into the chair beside her desk, his movements carrying the grace of decades of classical dance training. "In the dance of Nataraja, destruction and creation exist in perfect balance. Right now, my dear, you're stuck because you're trying to create without first destroying."

"Destroying what?"

"Your attachment to the outcome," he smiled, gesturing to her screen. "The ancient concept of 'vairagya' – it's like holding sand. The tighter you grasp..."

"The more it slips away," Maya finished, glancing at her email's eighth iteration.

Over the next week, Arun became Maya's guide in what he called "the dance of release." Each day brought a new lesson in letting go:

Day 1: The Prison of Attachment

"Watch your thoughts today," Arun instructed. "Notice how many are about controlling outcomes you can't actually control."

Maya tracked her mental patterns and was shocked to discover:

- She rewrote emails an average of 12 times
- Spent hours rehearsing conversations that never happened
- Repeatedly analyzed meetings from weeks ago
- Created detailed contingency plans for scenarios that never materialized

"This is what the texts mean by 'the mind being your worst enemy,'" Arun explained. "But it can also be your best friend – if you learn to hold it lightly."

Day 2: The Surrender Dance

Arun taught Maya a simple ritual. Before starting any task, she would write down her desired outcome on a small piece of paper, fold it, and place it in a beautiful box he gave her.

"Now," he said, "you dance with what's in front of you, not with what's in the box."

The effect was immediate. Without the weight of outcomes, her work began to flow naturally, like a river finding its course.

Day 3: The Witness Practice

"In dance," Arun shared, "we have something called 'sakshi bhava' – the witness consciousness. You're fully present but not entangled. Try it with your work."

Maya started setting a timer for 25 minutes, treating her tasks like a dance performance – fully engaged but not attached to perfection. Thoughts came and went like audience members, but she remained centered in her performance.

Day 4: Finding Flow

The breakthrough came unexpectedly. Maya was working on a major presentation when she noticed something different – time had disappeared, her movements between slides felt like choreography, and there was a natural rhythm to her work.

"Ah," Arun smiled when she described it, "you've found what the ancients called 'sahaja' – the natural state. Not forced, not controlled, just flowing."

As the weeks passed, Maya developed what she called her "Flow Formula":

1. Clear the Stage (Remove distractions, create sacred space)
2. Enter the Dance (Start without judgment, trust the rhythm)
3. Maintain the Movement (Stay present, release expectations)

She created simple rituals:

- Morning: Three deep breaths and the mantra "I release what I cannot control"
- Afternoon: Quick "flow checks" using the anchor of her breath
- Evening: Reviewing moments where flow happened naturally

The transformation was profound. Like the dance of Nataraja, destruction and creation found their balance. By destroying her need to control everything, she created space for natural flow.

One evening, Arun found her working late, but differently than before. Her movements were fluid, her expression peaceful.

"You've learned to dance with your work," he observed.

Maya smiled, finally understanding what he meant. "The email that started all this? I sent it after the second draft. And you know what? The world didn't end."

"And why would it?" Arun laughed. "The universe is already dancing perfectly. We just need to join in."

Your Dance Begins:

1. What are you gripping too tightly?
2. Can you feel the difference between effort and force?
3. What might flow naturally if you simply let go?

Remember: As the ancient texts say, "What you resist, persists. What you embrace, dissolves."

Are you ready to join the dance?

Summary:

- Maya, like many, struggles with the "chitta vritti" – the constant stream of thoughts and anxieties that hinder productivity and creativity.
- Arun, the dance teacher, introduces the concept of "vairagya" – detachment from the outcome. He emphasizes the importance of letting go of control and embracing the natural flow of work.
- Creating a conducive environment for focused work by minimizing distractions.
- Starting with intention and allowing the work to unfold naturally.
- Staying present and releasing the need for perfection.
- The Power of "Sahaja" (Natural Flow): By embracing the natural flow of work, Maya discovers a sense of ease and joy in her creative process.

Core Idea:

The core idea of the text revolves around the principle of "letting go" as a path to increased productivity and fulfillment. It emphasizes that by detaching from the need for control and embracing the natural flow of work, individuals can overcome the paralysis of perfectionism and achieve greater creativity and satisfaction.

Call to Action:

The text encourages readers to:

- Observe their own patterns of thought and identify areas where they are clinging to control.
- Practice "vairagya" by detaching from the outcome of their work.
- Create a conducive environment for focused work and embrace the natural flow of their creative process.
- Cultivate a mindset of "sahaja" – a state of effortless and joyful engagement with their work.

CHAPTER SEVEN

The Void Method in Practice

As the first rays of dawn painted the sky in hues of saffron, Arjun sat beneath the ancient banyan tree, his mind perfectly still. Like Lord Shiva in his cosmic dance of Tandava, he had learned to find rhythm in chaos, structure in emptiness. This was the Void Method in its purest form – not an absence of action, but a state of perfect balance between being and doing.

Daily Routines and Rituals

Consider the story of the great sage Vasishtha, who maintained his cosmic consciousness while fulfilling his worldly duties as a royal guru. Each morning, he would begin with the ritual of Surya Namaskar, not merely as physical exercise, but as a means to align his inner sun (consciousness) with the outer sun (universal energy). Similarly, the Void Method practitioner starts their day with intentional emptiness.

Morning Ritual Example:

- 5:30 AM: Rise before Brahma Muhurta (the cosmic hour)
- 5:45 AM: Pranayama (breath work) to clear the mental space
- 6:00 AM: Meditation in the void state
- 6:30 AM: Physical movement to integrate the void into the body

Integration Strategies for Work and Life

Like the cosmic dance of Nataraja, where Lord Shiva performs the five activities of creation, preservation, destruction, illusion, and emancipation simultaneously, the modern practitioner must learn to dance between various life domains while maintaining their center in the void.

Rama, even while ruling his kingdom, never lost his connection to the deeper reality. He demonstrated that one could be fully engaged in worldly duties while remaining inwardly untouched – the essence of karma yoga. This is the key to integrating the Void Method into a busy modern life.

Troubleshooting Common Challenges

The battlefield of Kurukshetra was shrouded in a tense stillness, broken only by the occasional clang of swords being sharpened and the muffled sounds of war drums. Amidst the vast armies, Arjuna, the mighty warrior and leader of the Pandavas, stood paralyzed by doubt. His hands trembled as he grasped his bow, Gandiva, and his heart was heavy with turmoil.

Before him stood his own family, friends, and teachers—people he loved and revered. To fight them felt like a betrayal of his soul, and yet to abandon the battle felt like a betrayal of his duty. Torn between these choices, Arjuna sank to his knees and declared to Krishna, his charioteer, "I cannot do this. How can I kill those I hold dear? My mind is clouded. What is the point of victory if it comes at such a cost?"

Krishna, ever serene and wise, listened patiently. He didn't rebuke Arjuna for his fear, nor did he command him to fight without question. Instead, Krishna smiled and began to speak, his voice steady and soothing, like the flow of a calm river.

"Arjuna," he said, "your despair stems not from the battle itself but from your attachment to its outcome. You see only loss and pain because you are clinging to the idea of what should be. But life does not pause for our fears. It asks us to act—not in pursuit of rewards or out of fear of failure, but because it is our dharma, our purpose."

Krishna's words were like a light cutting through the fog in Arjuna's mind. He explained the timeless wisdom of detachment. "The true warrior," Krishna said, "does not act out of desire for success or fear of defeat. He acts with clarity and focus, surrendering the results to a higher power. Your duty is to fight for righteousness, not to control the outcome. Let go of what you cannot control, and the path will reveal itself."

As Krishna's words sank in, Arjuna's heart grew lighter. He realized that his suffering was not caused by the battle, but by his resistance to it. By changing his perspective—by seeing his duty not as a burden but as an opportunity to grow—Arjuna found the courage to stand up once more.

When challenges arise in life, they are much like Arjuna's moment of doubt. The solution is not to run away from the battlefield but to transform how we perceive the fight. Just as Krishna taught Arjuna, we too can find clarity in action through detachment, embracing our purpose without being weighed down by fears of the outcome.

Picture the great sage Vasishtha sitting in meditation at twilight. Like many modern practitioners, he faced the three great obstacles that continue to challenge seekers today. Let us explore these challenges through his eyes:

The Thousand Whispers: Taming Mental Chatter

As Vasishtha sat beneath the stars, his mind buzzed like the thousand heads of Adisesha, each thought competing for attention. Just as this great cosmic serpent learned to focus all its heads to serve as Lord Vishnu's bed, Vasishtha discovered that the key wasn't to silence the thoughts but to give them all a single purpose.

A modern practitioner named Maya faced similar challenges during her high-pressure job as an emergency room doctor. Like Adisesha's thousand heads, the constant stream of patient information, medical procedures, and critical decisions threatened to overwhelm her. She learned to channel this mental chatter into a focused awareness, much like the serpent's heads aligned in service of the divine. Her technique? She visualized each thought as a head of the great serpent, all bowing in the same direction, serving her primary purpose: healing.

The Demon Dance: Transforming External Distractions

Consider the tale of sage Durvasa, whose meditation was constantly interrupted by demons sent to break his concentration. Rather than fighting them, he transformed their disruptions into opportunities for deeper practice. The louder they became, the more profound his silence grew.

Sarah, a mother of three young children, found her modern parallel in this ancient tale. Her home office, where she practiced the Void Method, was constantly invaded by little "demons" demanding attention, snacks, and resolution to sibling disputes. Like Durvasa, she learned to transform these interruptions into practice opportunities. Each distraction became a chance to demonstrate presence rather than resistance.

The Dance with Time: Mastering Rhythmic Living

The most formidable challenge came in the form of Kala, the deity of time itself. Legend tells of how Lord Shiva, in his Nataraja form, mastered time through his cosmic dance. Time wasn't to be conquered, but to be danced with.

James, a Silicon Valley executive, embodied this wisdom when facing crushing deadlines and packed schedules. Instead of fighting against time like an enemy, he learned to move with it like a dance partner. He structured his day not by rigid blocks but by rhythmic flows, much like the beats in Nataraja's drum. His meetings became opportunities for mindful engagement, his breaks became moments of conscious restoration, and even his commute transformed into a moving meditation.

The secret, as these practitioners discovered, wasn't in overpowering these challenges but in transforming their relationship with them. Like the great sages of old, they learned to turn obstacles into opportunities, distractions into devotion, and chaos into dance.

A contemporary practitioner, Dr. Amrita Patel, summarizes it beautifully: "The void doesn't eliminate our challenges; it gives us space to dance with them. In that dance, like Nataraja's cosmic movement, we find our freedom."

Long-term Maintenance and Growth

The story of sage Agastya, who drank the entire ocean but maintained it within himself, teaches us about containing vast experiences while remaining unchanged at our core. Long-term practitioners of the Void Method develop this same capacity – to engage fully with life while maintaining their connection to emptiness.

As we conclude this chapter, remember that like the eternal dance of Nataraja, your practice of the Void Method is both ever-changing and changeless.

Summary:

- Establishing a morning routine with practices like pranayama and meditation helps to cultivate inner stillness and prepare for the day.

- The Void Method can be integrated into all aspects of life, including work, relationships, and social interactions.
- Examples include finding presence in challenging situations (like Rama's leadership) and embracing interruptions as opportunities for practice (like Durvasa).
- Channeling mental activity into a focused direction, like a serpent's heads aligning.
- Viewing distractions as opportunities for practice, like Durvasa transforming demon interruptions into deeper meditation.
- Moving with the flow of time, like Nataraja's dance, rather than resisting it.
- Cultivating the ability to engage fully with life while maintaining inner stillness, like Agastya containing the ocean within himself.

Core Idea:

The core idea is that the Void Method is not about escaping from life but about finding a state of profound presence and balance within the midst of it. It's about:

- Cultivating inner stillness: Through practices like meditation and pranayama.
- Integrating this stillness into daily life: By finding presence in all activities, from work to relationships.
- Transforming challenges into opportunities for growth: By responding to distractions and obstacles with equanimity and grace.

- Maintaining a deep connection to the void while fully engaged in the world: Like Nataraja dancing, finding harmony between action and stillness.

Call to Action:

The text encourages readers to:

- Incorporate daily practices like meditation and pranayama into their routines.
- Find ways to integrate the Void Method into their work, relationships, and daily life.
- Cultivate awareness of their mental patterns and learn to respond to distractions with equanimity.
- Embrace the challenges of life as opportunities for growth and transformation.

CHAPTER EIGHT

Beyond Procrastination: Dancing with the Void

Long ago, before time and space existed, there was only an endless void—vast, silent, and still. This void was neither dark nor light, neither full nor empty. It simply *was*. For eons, it existed in perfect equilibrium, holding the potential for everything but manifesting nothing.

One day, a wandering soul—a spark of curiosity—drifted into this void. It marveled at the stillness, but after a time, it began to feel restless. "There's nothing here," the spark said to itself. "Only emptiness. No stars to admire, no worlds to explore, no companions to share my thoughts. Why does this void even exist if it offers nothing?"

The void, though silent, seemed to hear. And in its infinite stillness, it responded—not with words, but with a subtle pulse. The spark felt this pulse as an invitation, a whisper that seemed to say, *"Look closer."*

Intrigued, the spark quieted its complaints and began to observe the void more deeply. As it did, something remarkable happened. The void was no longer just an absence—it began to shimmer with potential. Within its infinite silence, the spark saw the faint outlines of worlds waiting to be born. It realized that the void wasn't empty at all; it was brimming with possibility, like a blank canvas longing for an artist's brush.

The spark reached out, drawing from the void with its own imagination. From its touch, light blossomed, creating stars that danced across the expanse. With each new thought, more forms emerged: planets spun into existence, oceans began to swell, and life awakened. The void, once thought barren, had become the birthplace of creation itself.

As the spark continued to create, it had a revelation. "The void is not nothingness," it said. "It is the source of *everything*. Without its silence, there could be no sound. Without its stillness, no movement. Its emptiness is not a lack—it is the foundation."

And so, the spark continued its dance with the void, shaping and reshaping existence. It understood now that the void was not its adversary but its partner, offering infinite freedom to imagine, to create, to become.

In the same way, your relationship with emptiness can transform your life. When faced with moments of stillness or absence, do not fear the void. Embrace it. See it not as emptiness, but as the fertile soil where the seeds of your greatest creativity can grow. Like the spark, you too can draw from the infinite possibilities within the void—and create something extraordinary.

Maya stood at the floor-to-ceiling windows of her office, watching the sun paint the sky in brilliant oranges and pinks. Six months had passed since she first began her journey with the void. Her desk, once cluttered with half-finished projects and sticky note reminders, now held only her laptop, showing a single window. The silence in her office felt different now - not the heavy quiet of procrastination, but the pregnant pause before creation.

"Remember when this space used to terrify you?" a familiar voice asked.

Maya turned to find Arun, her mentor in both dance and life, standing in her doorway. His presence always reminded her of how far she'd come.

"I used to fill every moment with noise," she admitted, gesturing to her now-silent phone. "I thought emptiness meant something was wrong."

Arun smiled, settling into the chair by her desk. "Ah, like Shiva's cosmic dance - the Tandava. Creation needs destruction, just as clarity needs emptiness. Show me what you've learned."

Maya opened her journal, its pages filled with six months of insights:

Month 1: Dancing with Fear

"I was terrified of empty space," Maya read from her early entries. "I'd open sixteen tabs the moment I sat down, check emails compulsively, anything to avoid the void."

"And now?" Arun asked.

Maya gestured to her single open window. "Now I understand what you meant about 'marma' - finding strength in apparent weakness. The emptiness isn't my enemy anymore; it's my power source."

Month 2: The First Steps

She flipped to another page. "This was when you taught me about 'Rita' - cosmic order. I started noticing my natural rhythms:"

- Morning void: 30 minutes of emptiness before opening any devices
- Creation blocks: 90 minutes of focused work
- Integration spaces: 15 minutes of conscious pause between tasks

"Like a dancer finding their rhythm," Arun nodded approvingly.

Month 3: The Breakthrough

"This was the hardest month," Maya recalled. "Everything was falling apart - or so I thought."

Arun chuckled. "Ah, when you discovered true 'Shunyata'?"

"Yes. My biggest project had just failed. Instead of rushing to fix it, I let myself sit in the emptiness. And then, like magic..."

"Not magic," Arun corrected. "Natural law. Like the Upanishads teach: 'From fullness, take fullness away, and fullness remains.'"

Month 4: The New Dance

Maya's journal entries showed a shift:

- Fewer projects, greater impact
- Less busy, more productive
- Reduced stress, increased creativity

"I started teaching my team about void spaces," Maya shared. "At first, they thought I was crazy. Empty time on their calendars? Meditation before meetings? But then they saw the results."

Month 5: The Integration

"This is when everything changed," Maya said, pointing to a particular entry. "I stopped seeing the void as something to schedule and started seeing it as the foundation of everything."

Her new approach emerged:

1. Sacred Empty Time: Like the space between musical notes
2. Focused Creation: Like a dancer in perfect flow
3. Conscious Completion: Like the final pose in a performance

Month 6: The Teaching

"And now?" Arun asked, though his smile suggested he already knew.

Maya walked him to her office's glass wall, where a new organizational chart hung. Instead of the traditional hierarchy, it showed rhythmic cycles of creation and void, activity and rest, doing and being.

"We've transformed how we work," she explained. "Our team productivity is up 40%, but more importantly, people are thriving. They've found their own relationships with emptiness."

Arun stood beside her, watching the sunset paint the sky. "You know what this reminds me of?"

"The void before creation," they said together, laughing.

"You've learned well," Arun said softly. "But remember what the Yoga Vasishtha says..."

"'What appears to be emptiness to the ignorant is fullness to the wise,'" Maya finished. "I'm still learning. Every day, the void teaches me something new."

As if on cue, her phone lit up with an urgent message. The old Maya would have jumped to answer it. The new Maya smiled, let it sit in the void, and turned back to the sunset.

"Ready for your next lesson?" Arun asked, his eyes twinkling.

Maya looked at her empty desk, her quiet phone, her single open window, and felt the infinite potential humming in the spaces between.

"Always," she answered. "The void has so much more to teach."

Your Dance with the Void Begins:

1. What spaces in your life are asking to be emptied?
2. Where might stillness serve better than action?
3. What creativity waits in your personal void?

Remember: Like the cosmic dance of creation, your journey with emptiness is eternal. What will you create from your void today?

Summary:

- The story begins with the concept of the void as the source of all creation. It emphasizes that emptiness is not nothingness but a space of infinite potential.
- Cultivating moments of quiet reflection and introspection.
- Integrating periods of focused work with periods of intentional emptiness.
- Surrendering to the natural flow of life and embracing uncertainty.
- The text demonstrates how creating space in various aspects of life – physical, mental, and digital – can lead to increased creativity, productivity, and overall well-being.
- The text emphasizes that the void is not something to fear but a fertile ground for personal and professional growth.

Core Idea:

The core idea of the text is that embracing emptiness is not about inaction but about cultivating a deeper connection to oneself and the universe. It's about finding the space for creativity, insight, and true fulfillment. The void is not a void at all, but a source of infinite potential, waiting to be explored and expressed.

Call to Action:

The text encourages readers to:

- Cultivate moments of stillness in their daily lives through practices like meditation, deep breathing, and spending time in nature.
- Create space in their physical and digital environments by decluttering and minimizing distractions.
- Embrace periods of emptiness as opportunities for reflection, creativity, and inner growth.
- Recognize that the void is not a lack but a source of infinite potential.

CHAPTER NINE

Conclusion: The Sacred Dance of Emptiness

The Final Movement

Like the divine dance of Nataraja, our journey through the void comes full circle. Each step we've taken—from confronting emptiness to discovering its creative potential—echoes the universe's own rhythm of creation and dissolution. Just as the cosmic dancer's drum beats to the rhythm of existence, our exploration of the void has revealed a profound truth: what we once feared as emptiness is actually the birthplace of all possibility.

Consider Maya's transformation one final time. She sits at her desk, no longer surrounded by the chaos of notifications and endless tabs, but embraced by a powerful stillness. The same space that once filled her with anxiety now pulses with creative potential. Her journey mirrors the ancient wisdom of the Upanishads: within apparent emptiness lies the seed of all creation.

The Sacred Marriage of Wisdom

Like Ardhanarishvara—Shiva's half-male, half-female form—our journey has united seemingly opposite truths:

- Emptiness and fullness
- Surrender and power
- Stillness and movement
- Destruction and creation

Through Maya's story, we've witnessed how these apparent opposites dance together in perfect harmony. Her cleared desk became not a symbol of lack but a canvas of possibility. Her released attachments transformed into wings of freedom. Her embraced uncertainties blossomed into unprecedented creativity.

The Four Pillars of Void Wisdom

In a serene valley cradled by misty mountains, there lived a wandering seeker named Ayan. Ayan was restless, carrying within him a gnawing void—a sense of emptiness he couldn't escape. He had traveled far and wide, seeking meaning in temples, scriptures, and teachers, but no wisdom seemed to fill the hollow ache within him. One evening, as the sun dipped below the horizon, he stumbled upon an ancient hermitage hidden in the woods.

An old sage emerged from the shadows, his eyes gleaming with timeless clarity. Sensing Ayan's turmoil, he said, "You carry the void as a burden, but what if it is a gift? To master it, you must embrace the Four Pillars of Void Wisdom. Stay here, and you shall learn."

1. Sukshma Darshan (The Subtle Vision)

The sage led Ayan to a still lake under the moonlight. "Gaze into the water," the sage instructed. "What do you see?"

"Nothing," Ayan replied, his voice tinged with frustration.

"Look deeper," the sage urged.

As Ayan focused, the surface ripples stilled, and he began to see the reflection of the moon and stars. Then, beneath the surface, he noticed the faint movement of fish and the shimmer of unseen life.

"In the void of the water, infinite life dances," said the sage. "The same is true of your emptiness. Every silence holds a symphony waiting to be heard. Every pause hides potential. Learn to see the unseen, and you will find treasures in the void."

Ayan began to see his empty moments differently—not as barren wastelands, but as fertile grounds for growth.

2. Tyaga Shakti (The Power of Release)

Next, the sage handed Ayan a heavy satchel filled with stones. "Carry this," he said, and led him up a steep hill.

With each step, Ayan's burden grew heavier, and his frustration mounted. Halfway up, he cried, "I cannot go on like this!"

"Then let go of what you don't need," the sage replied.

Ayan hesitated, but as he began to discard stones, his load lightened. By the time he reached the peak, he carried only a single stone—a reminder of what truly mattered.

"Kali teaches us to sever what doesn't serve," said the sage. "Release your distractions, your need for perfection, your attachment to outcomes. In letting go, you make space for clarity, flow, and power in the present."

Ayan felt freer than he ever had, realizing how much unnecessary weight he had been carrying in his mind and heart.

3. Sakshi Bhava (The Witness Presence)

At dawn, the sage brought Ayan to a raging river. "Step into the water," he said.

Ayan waded in, struggling to stay upright as the current tugged at him. He grabbed at branches and rocks, but the more he fought, the more he was pulled under.

"Stop fighting!" the sage called. "Be the witness, not the struggler."

Ayan stopped resisting and allowed himself to float. To his amazement, he found balance amidst the chaos, letting the current carry him instead of battling it.

"Life is ever-changing," the sage said from the riverbank. "Like the unchanging consciousness that watches the dance of life, learn to remain steady in uncertainty. In chaos, find your balance. In structure, embrace spontaneity. The witness is always free."

Ayan emerged from the river with a newfound calm, understanding that he could face life's turbulence without being swept away.

4. Srijan Kala (The Art of Creation)

Finally, the sage handed Ayan a lump of clay. "Shape this," he instructed.

At first, Ayan hesitated, overwhelmed by the blankness of the clay. But as he began to work, his hands moved with intuition, creating a delicate lotus.

The sage smiled. **"From the void, Brahma creates. From your emptiness, you too can bring forth beauty and meaning. Channel your creative force. Build not for perfection, but from your truth. Sustainable practices emerge when you create from alignment, not obligation."**

As the morning light illuminated his creation, Ayan realized that his emptiness had been a gift all along—a source of endless potential waiting to be expressed.

Ayan stayed in the hermitage for many moons, mastering the Four Pillars of Void Wisdom. When he finally returned to the world, he was no longer burdened by the void but empowered by it. In the pauses of life, he saw infinite possibility. In letting go, he found clarity. In chaos, he stood steady. And from the depths of his emptiness, he created a life of meaning, balance, and beauty.

The Eternal Dance

Remember the story of Abhimanyu from the Mahabharata—he knew how to enter the Chakravyuha but not how to navigate within it. Many of us began this journey similarly, knowing we needed to enter the void but uncertain of what lay beyond. Now we understand both the steps and the spaces between them.

Your ongoing practice might include:

Daily Rhythm

- Begin with sacred emptiness
- Practice the void pause
- End with grateful reflection

Weekly Integration

- Review your relationship with empty spaces
- Notice where resistance arises
- Celebrate moments of flow

Monthly Expansion

- Explore new applications
- Deepen understanding
- Share insights

The Final Movement

Like the space between breaths, between thoughts, between moments—your void awaits. Not as an emptiness to be feared, but as the canvas of infinite possibility. Remember Maya's journey from resistance to flow, from fear to freedom. Your path may look different, but the wisdom remains the same: within your deepest emptiness lies your greatest potential.

As Shiva's cosmic dance reminds us—destruction and creation are not opposites, but partners in the eternal dance of becoming. Each time you face the void, you join this sacred movement. Each moment of surrender becomes a moment of power. Each empty space becomes a birthplace of possibility.

The journey never truly ends. Like the endless dance of creation, it simply takes new forms, reveals new depths, opens new doors. You've learned to see the power in pauses, the creativity in silence, the strength in surrender. Now it's time to dance your own dance, to create your own rhythm, to transform your own emptiness into endless possibility.

The void is not just calling you—it's waiting for you. Not as an end, but as a beginning. Not as an absence, but as a presence. Not as a void to be filled, but as a space to be danced in.

Step in. Breathe deep. Let go.

The dance is already within you.

ॐ शून्यता पूरणता एकम् (Om Shunyata Purnata Ekam) The Void and the Fullness are One

ॐ शांति शांति शांति: (Om Shanti Shanti Shanti)

Afterword: A Personal Note To Readers

Dear Fellow Seeker,

As we conclude our exploration of the Void, I find myself reflecting on the profound journey we've shared through these pages. In many ways, this ending is just the beginning—your beginning. The true test of any wisdom lies not in its reading, but in its living.

We live in an age of unprecedented distraction. Our phones buzz with endless notifications, social media feeds scroll infinitely, and short-form content like reels and TikToks fragment our attention into ever-smaller pieces. Each notification, each scroll, each quick dopamine hit slowly erodes the sacred space within us where genuine creativity, purpose, and peace reside.

But you've already taken the first step by recognizing this pattern. By picking up this book, you've shown a readiness to reclaim your time, your attention, and ultimately, your life's direction. You're ready to transform from a passive consumer of endless content into an active creator of your own destiny.

Remember that your svadharma—your personal duty and life's purpose—cannot be found in the endless scroll of social media or the reactive cycles of digital distraction. It emerges from the very void we've learned to embrace, from the quiet moments of reflection and genuine self-connection.

As you move forward from these pages, be gentle with yourself. The path of transformation is not linear. There will be days when old habits resurface, when the pull of distraction feels overwhelming. This is natural. What matters is not perfection, but the consistent return to awareness, the willingness to begin again.

Consider starting small:

- Create pockets of silence in your day, even if just for five minutes
- Notice the urge to reach for your phone without acting on it
- Practice sitting with uncertainty instead of filling it with noise
- Observe how your energy shifts when you choose presence over distraction

Your journey with the Void is uniquely yours. While the principles we've explored are universal, how you apply them will be deeply personal. Trust this process. Trust yourself. The very emptiness that once frightened you will become your greatest source of strength and clarity.

Remember, every moment you choose presence over distraction, mindfulness over mindless scrolling, and purpose over passive consumption, you're not just changing your habits—you're changing your life's trajectory.

The world needs your unique gifts, your authentic voice, your true presence. Not the filtered, curated version of yourself that social media demands, but the raw, real, evolving human being that you are. Your journey through the Void will help you uncover and express these gifts.

I invite you to stay connected with this work, not through endless social media updates, but through deep, practical implementation in your daily life. Let the principles we've explored take root in your routine, your decisions, your way of being.

The path ahead is both challenging and beautiful. You'll find that the more you embrace the Void, the more it gives back—in clarity, in purpose, in authentic achievement. You're not just learning to manage procrastination; you're learning to live more fully, more authentically, more purposefully.